This book
belongs to

_____

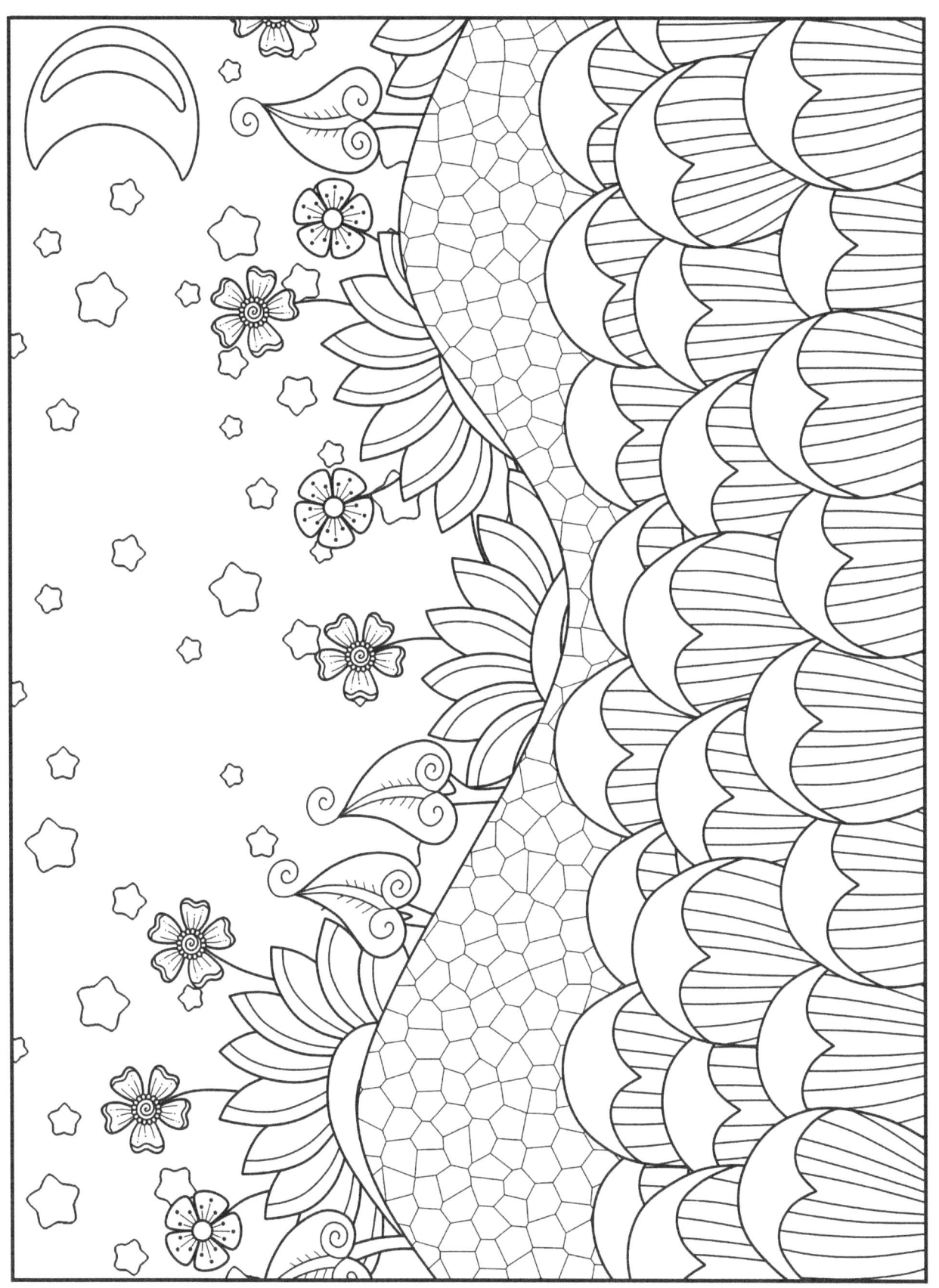

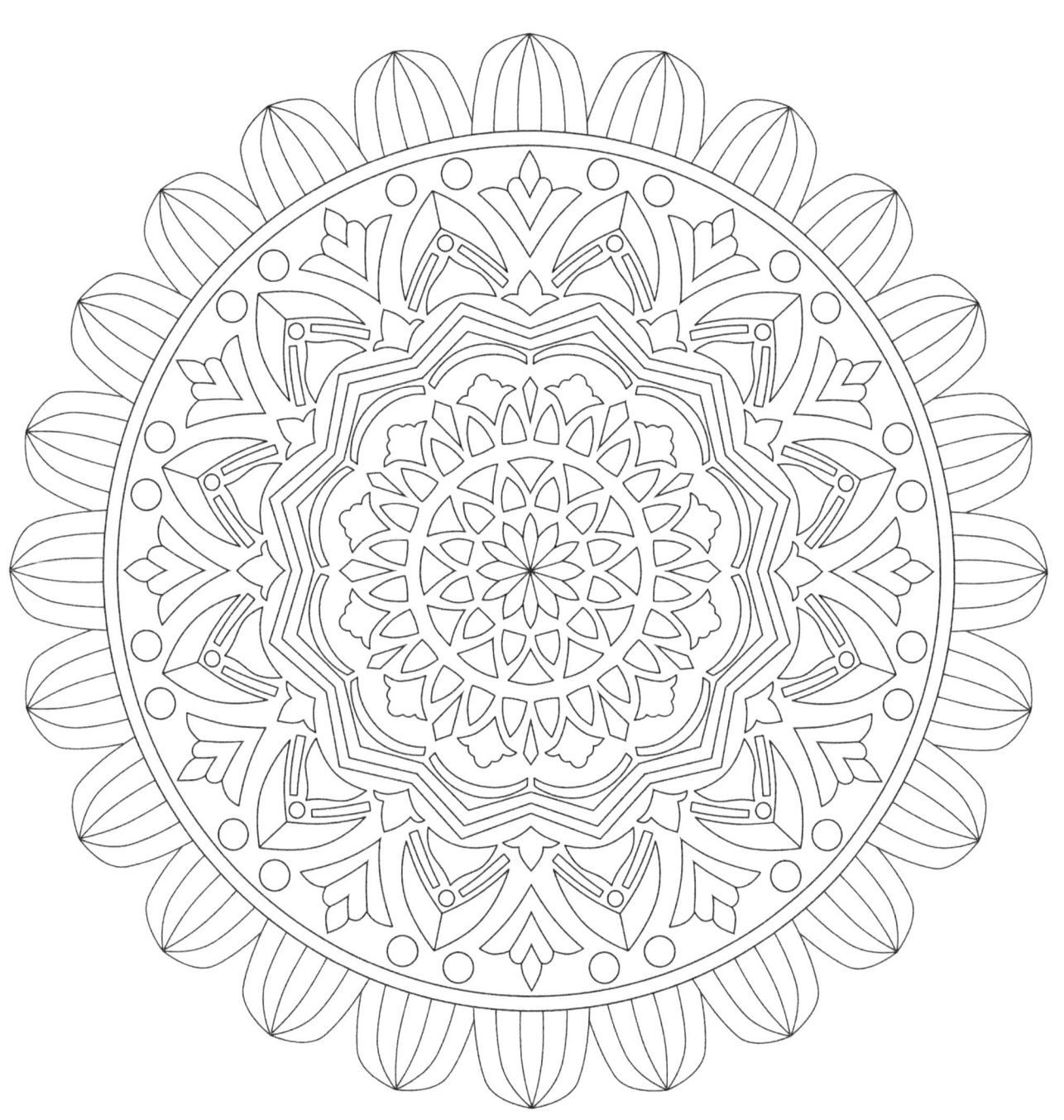

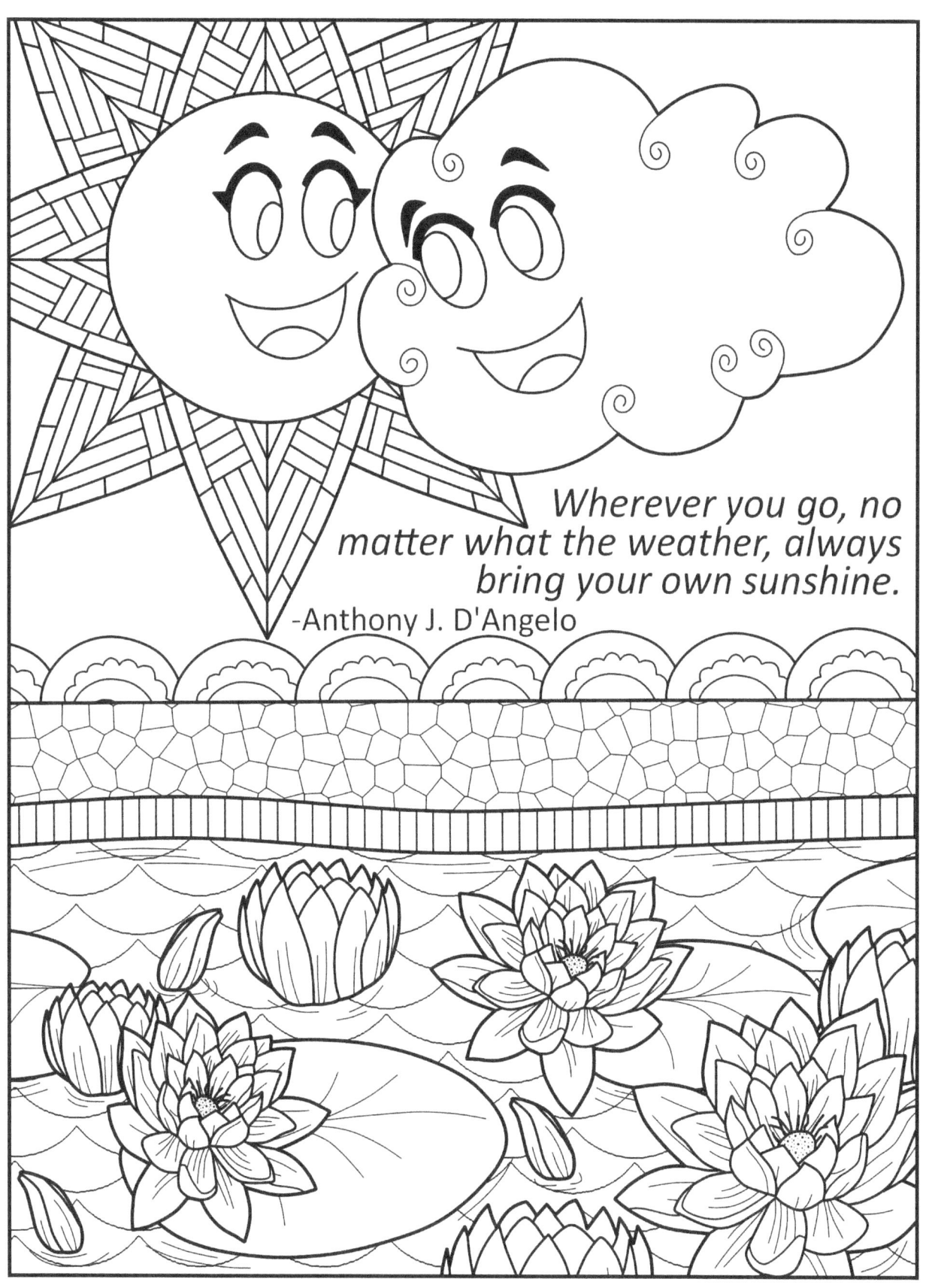

Wherever you go, no matter what the weather, always bring your own sunshine.
-Anthony J. D'Angelo

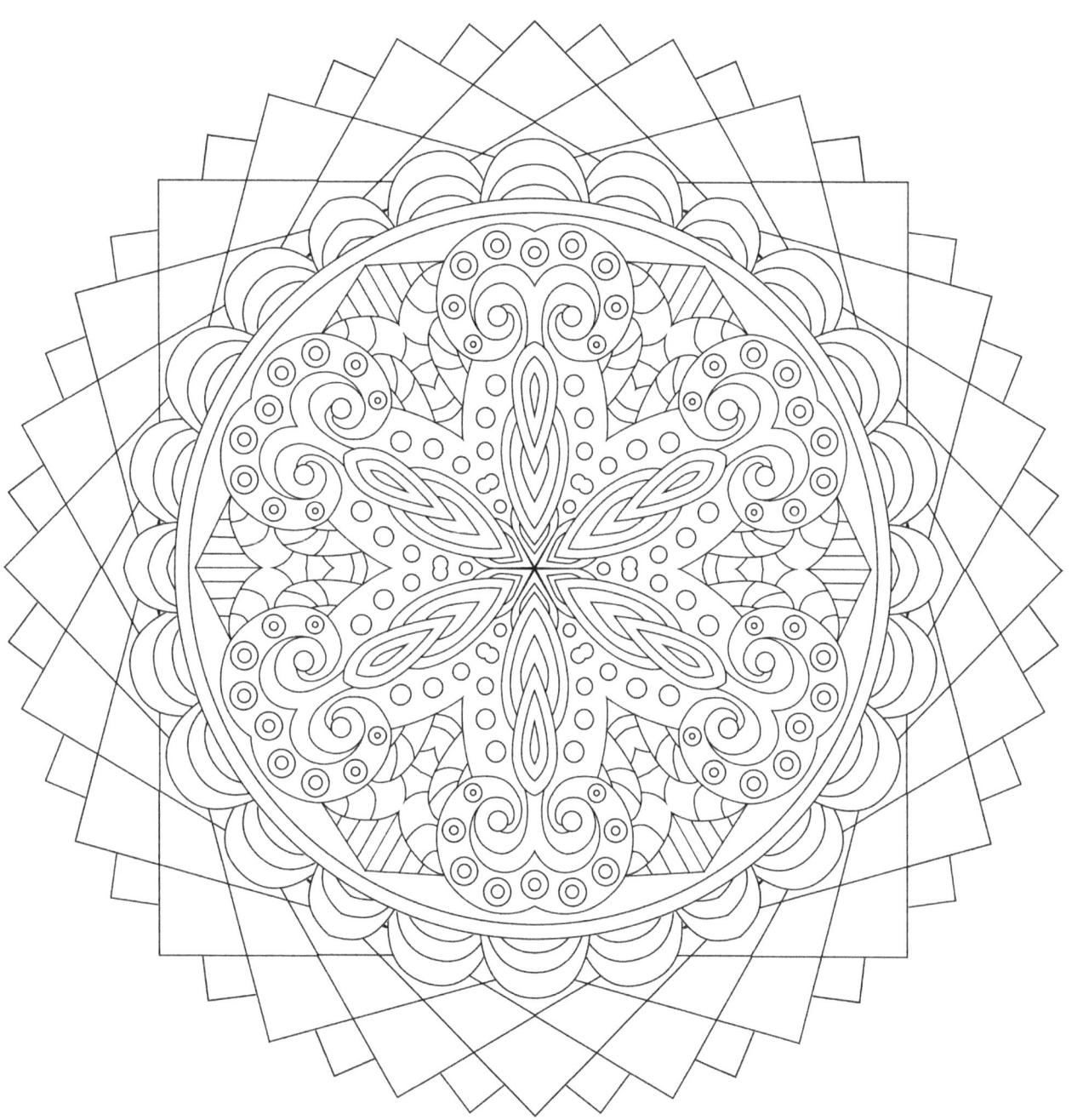

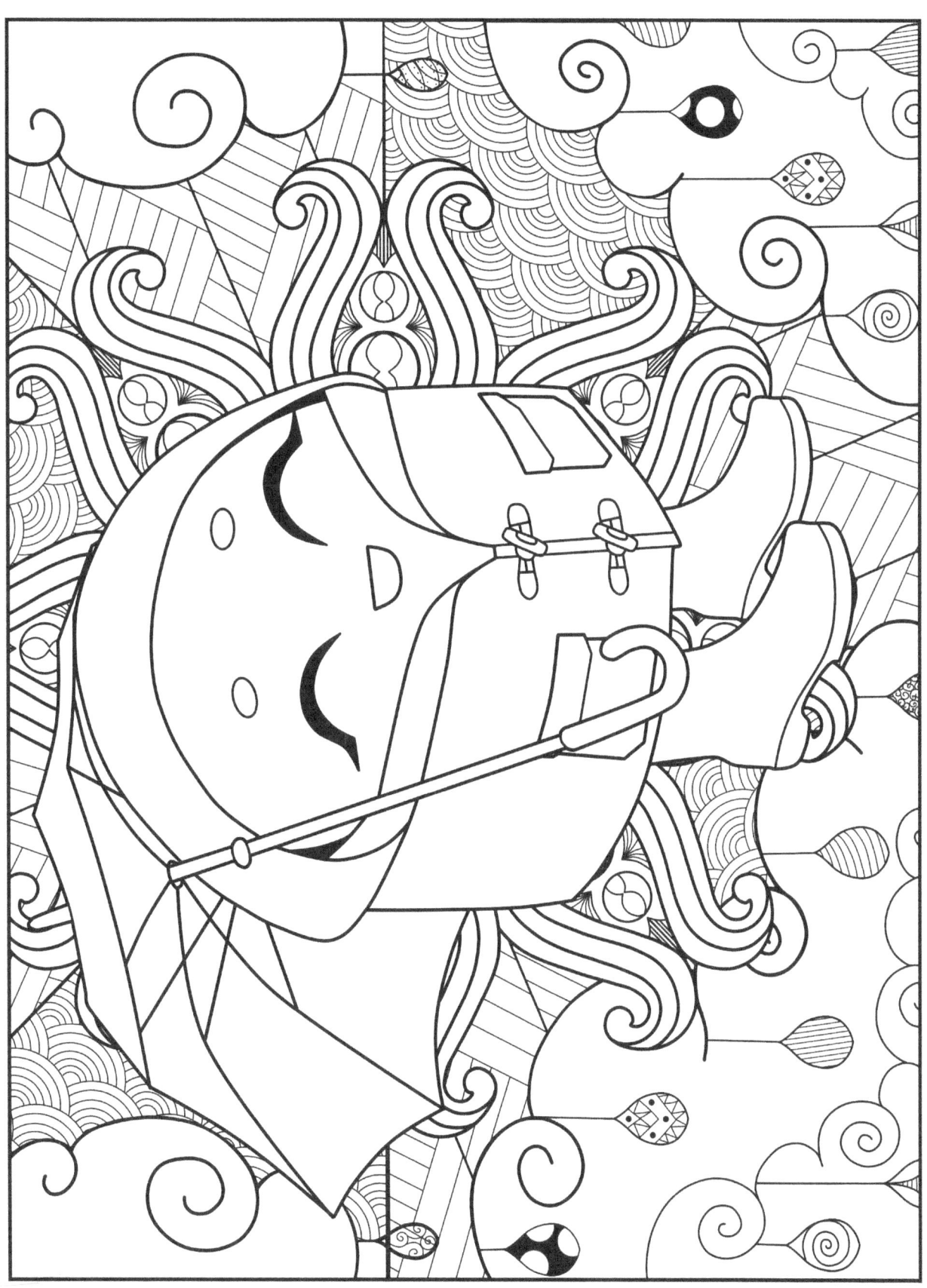

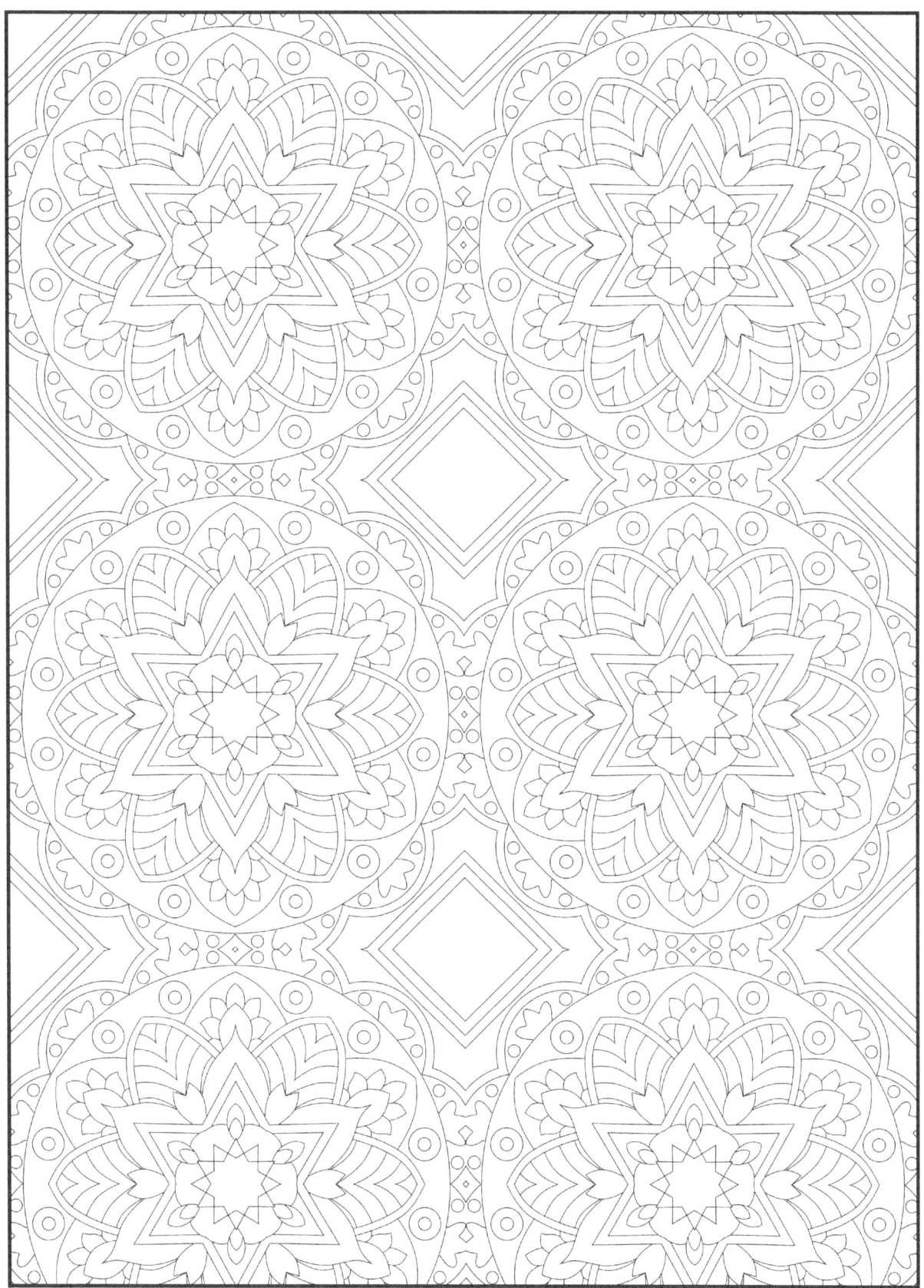

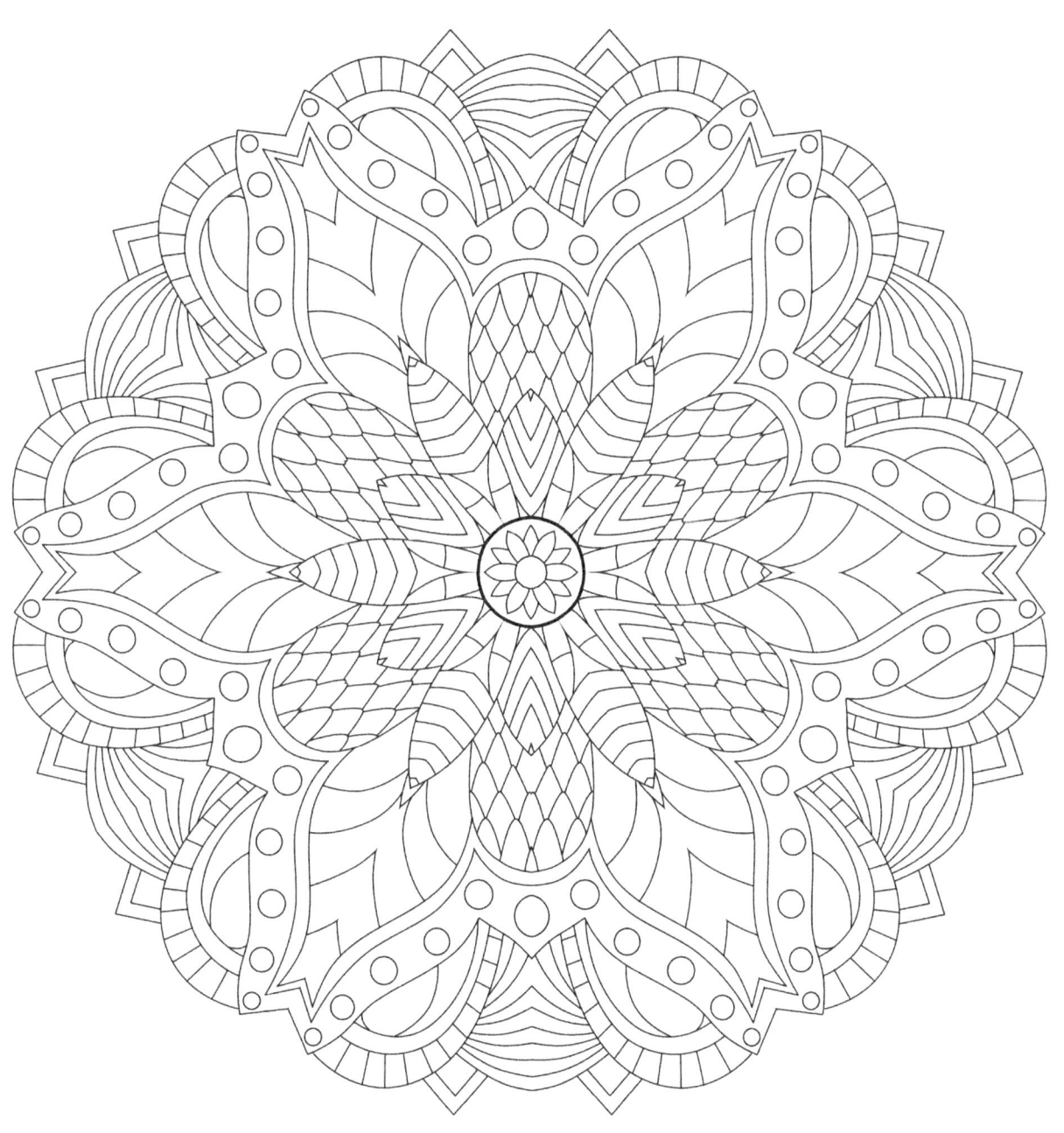

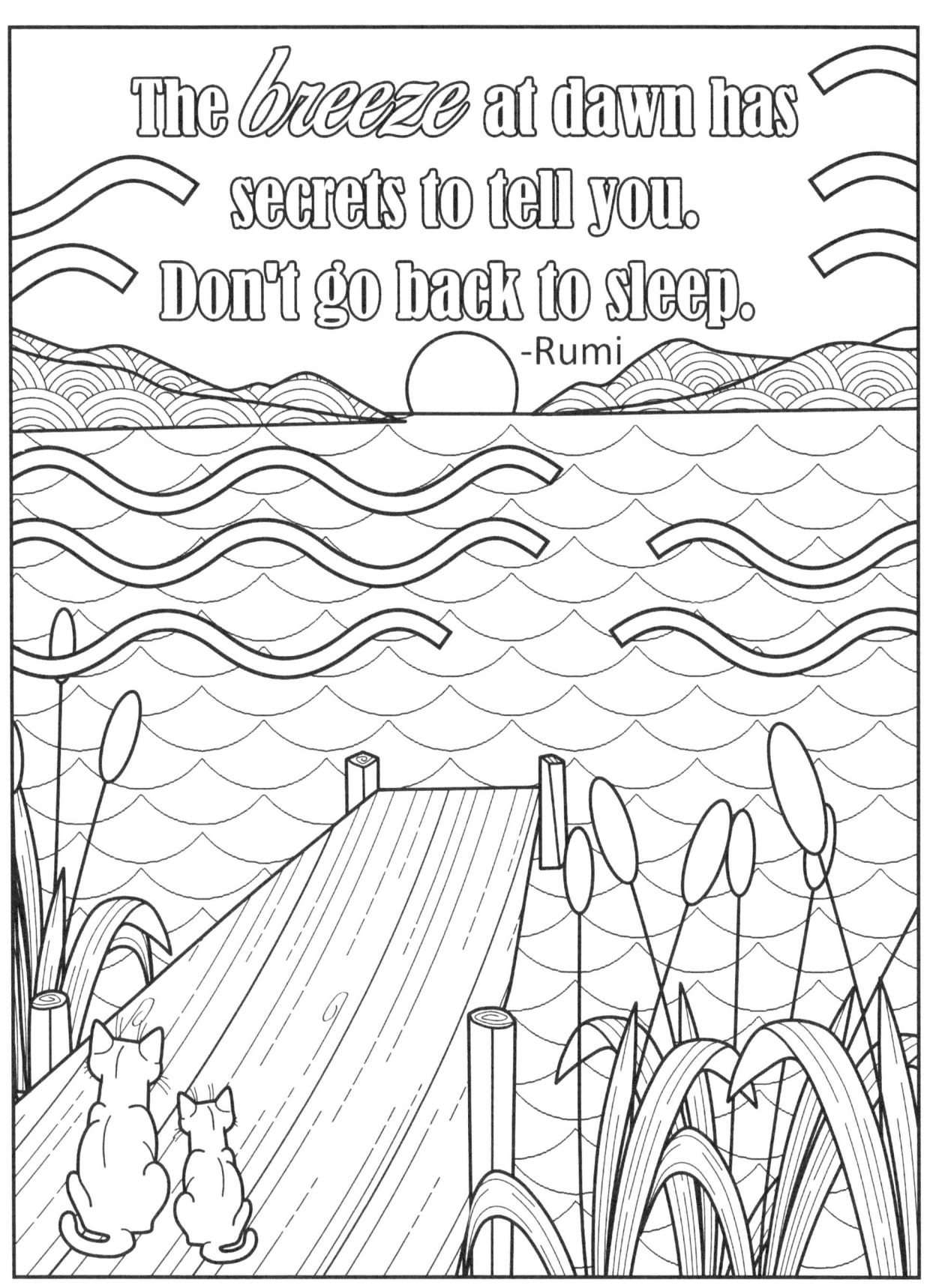

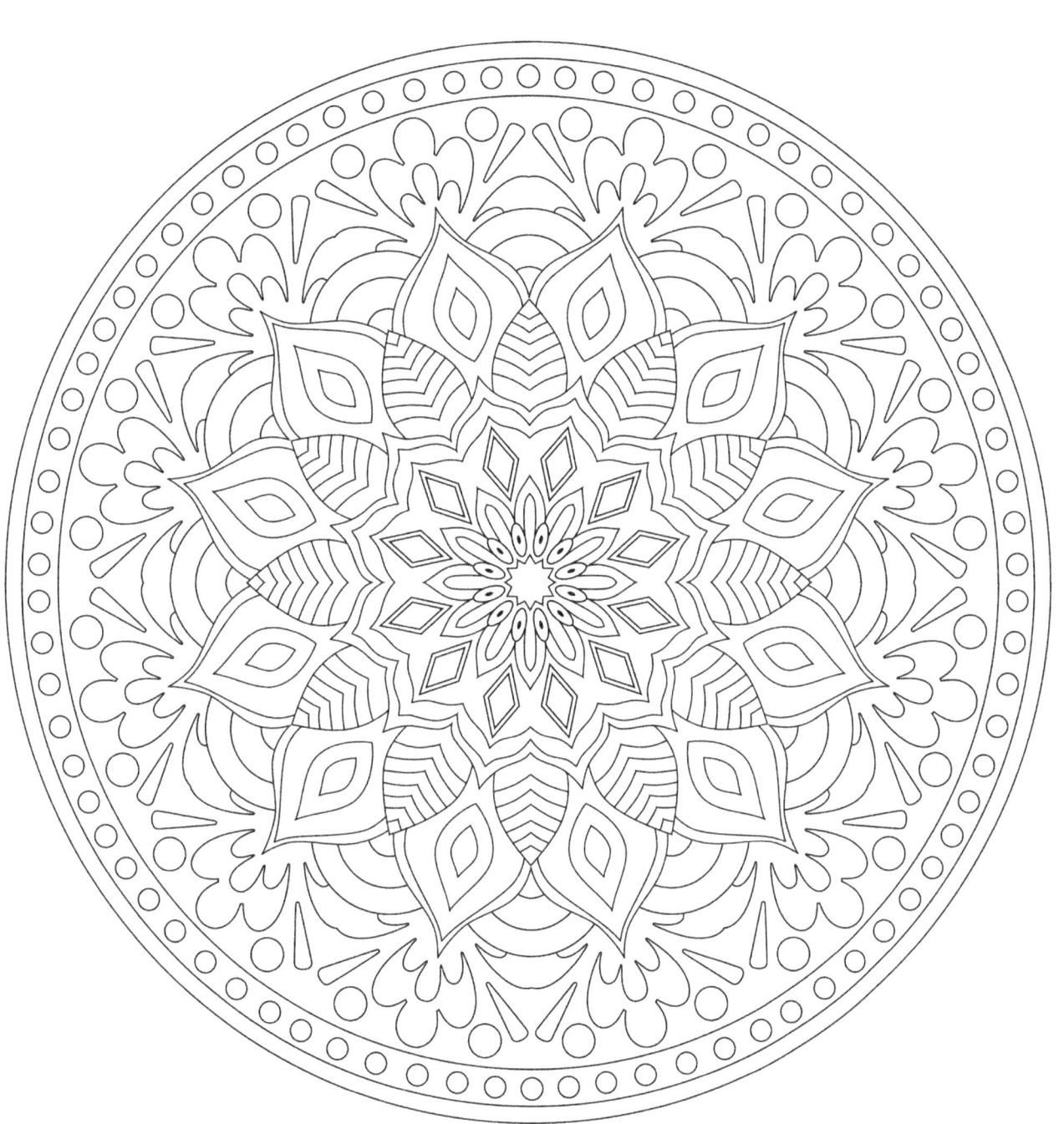

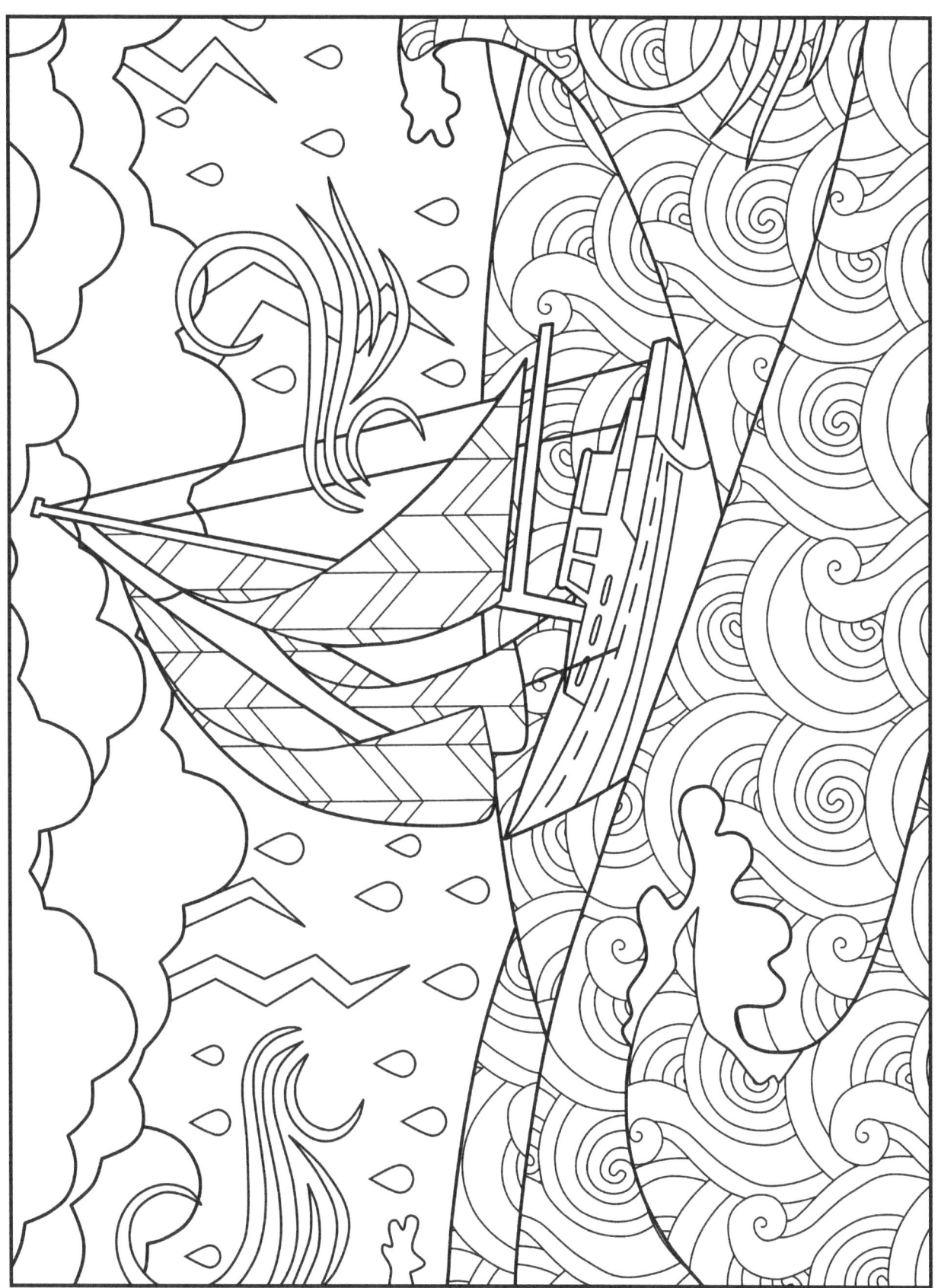

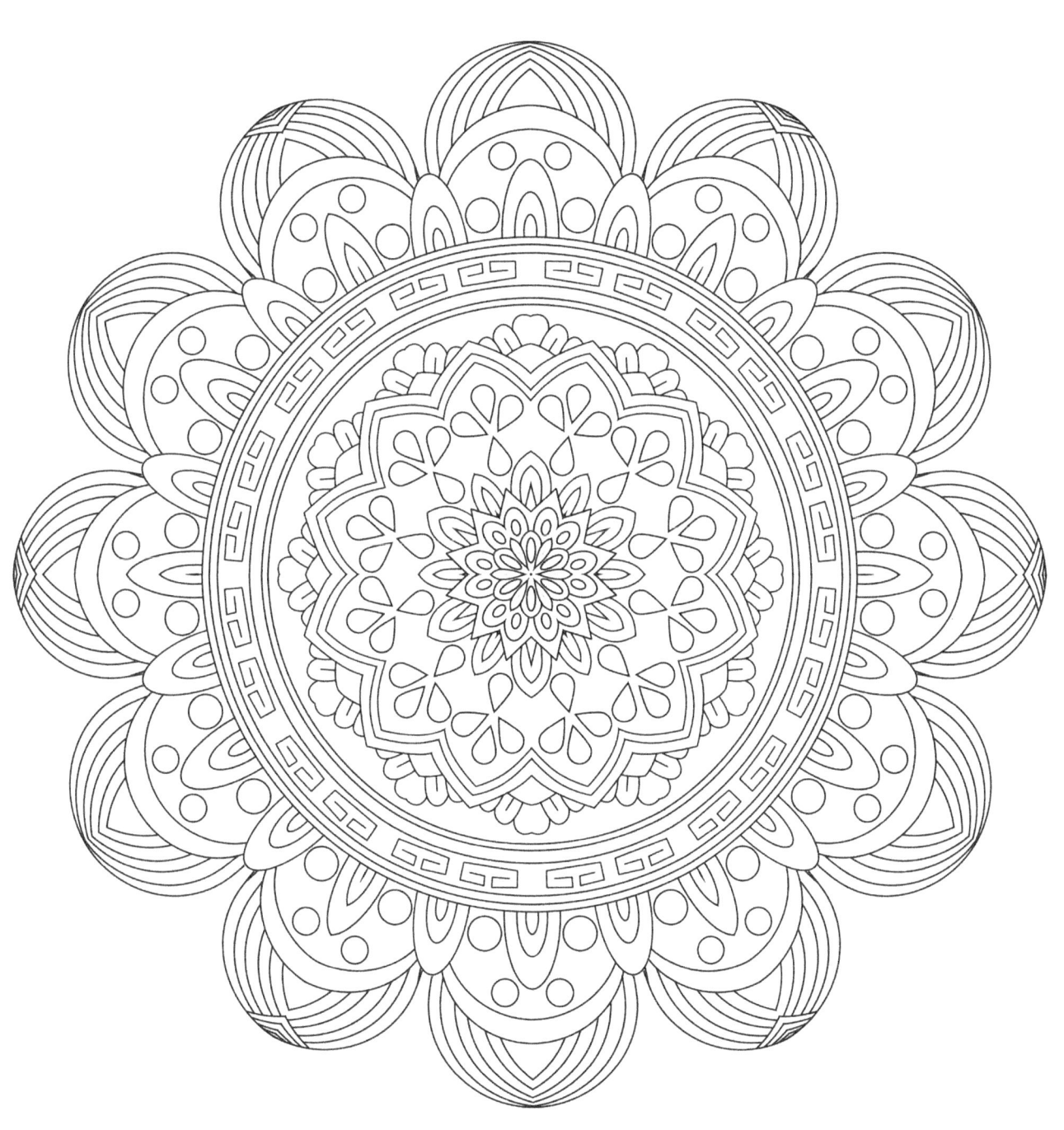

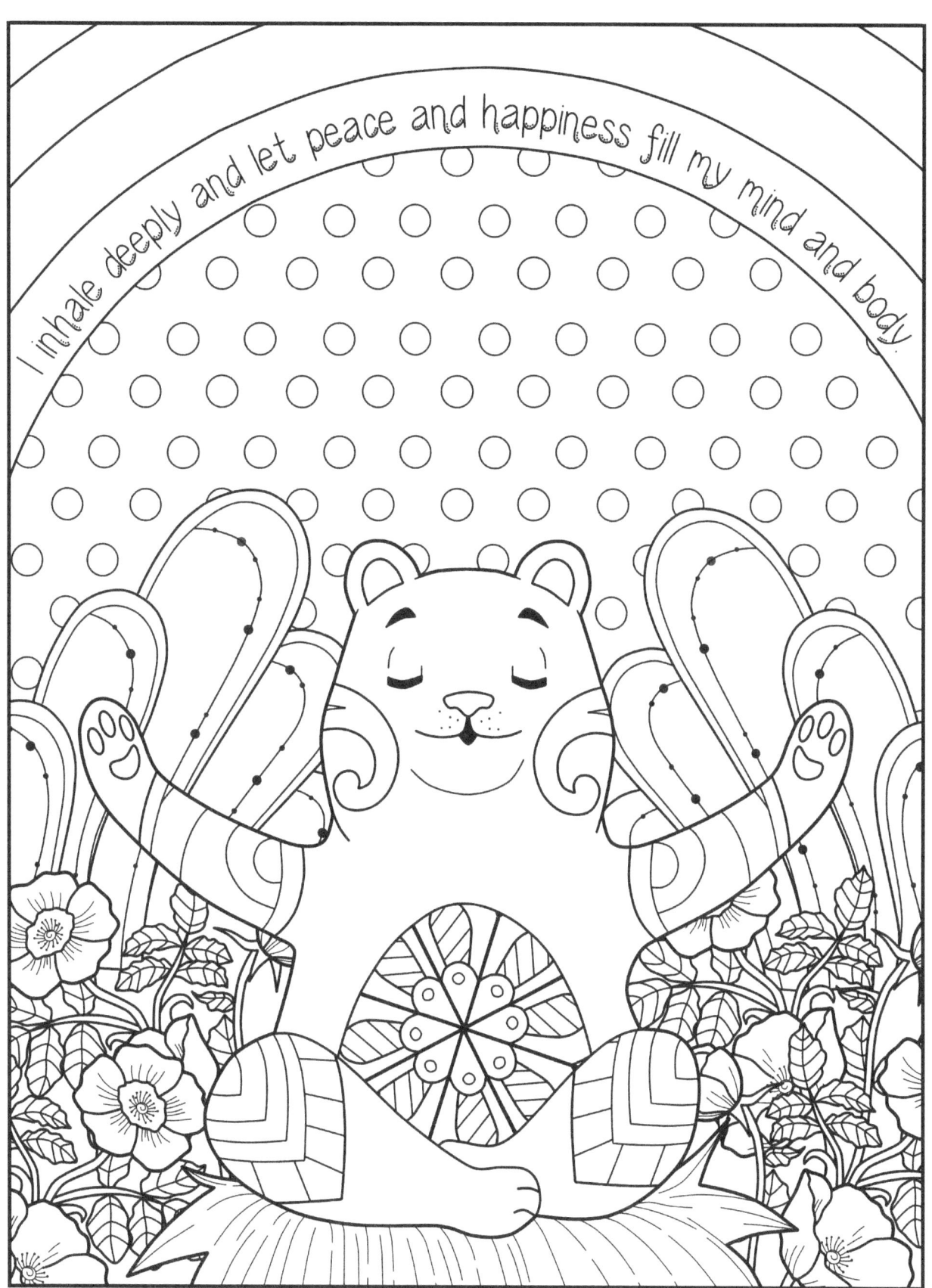

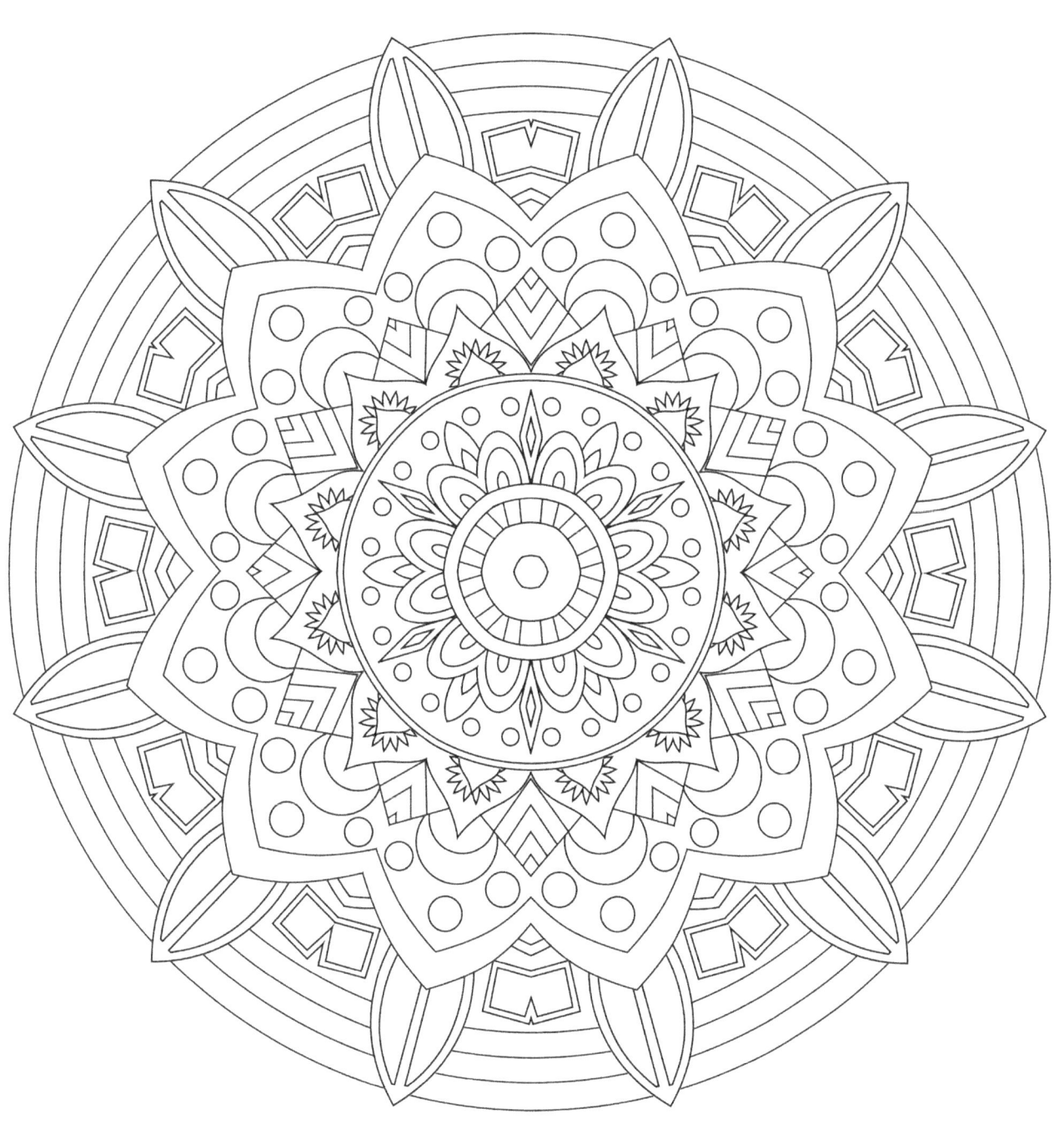

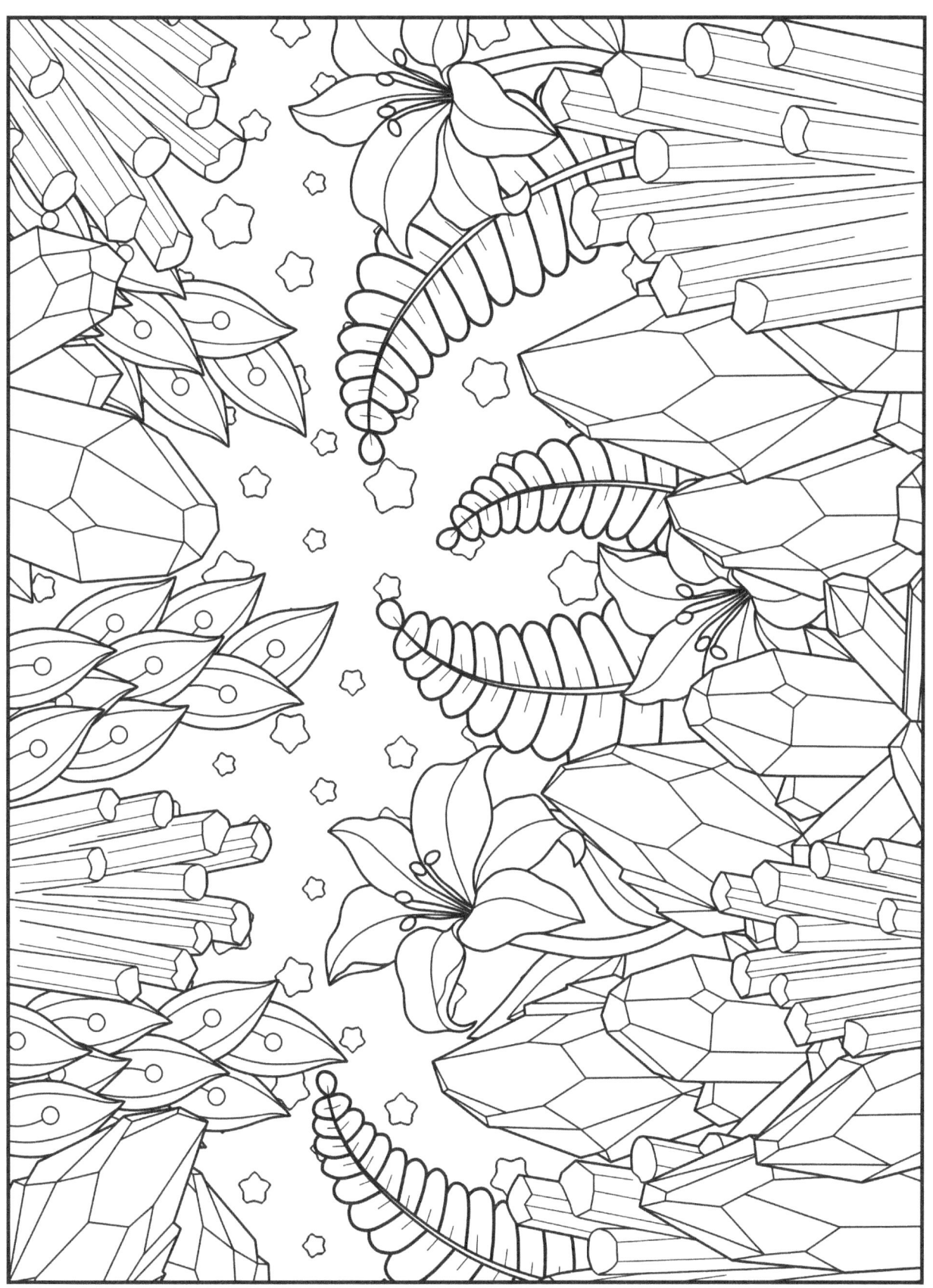

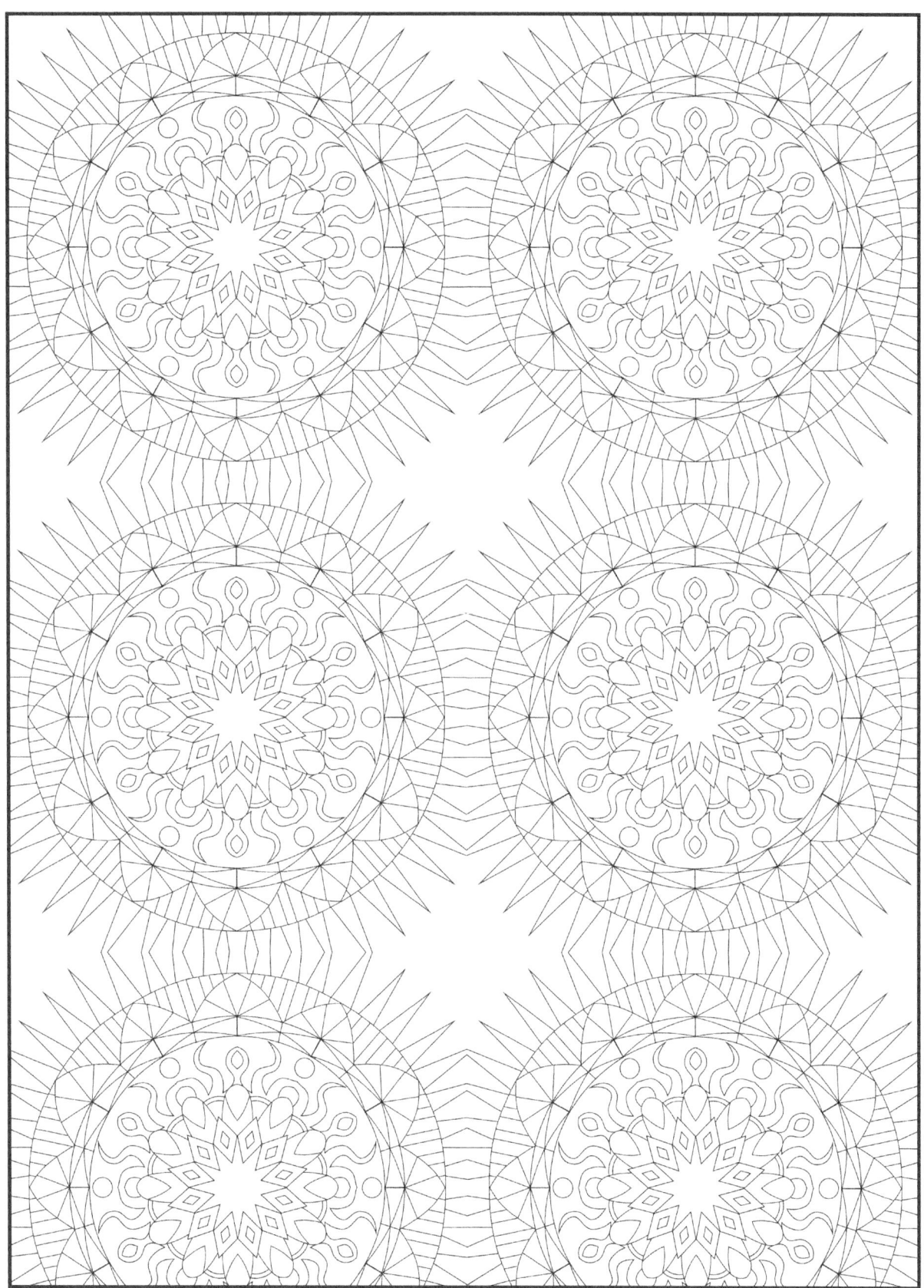

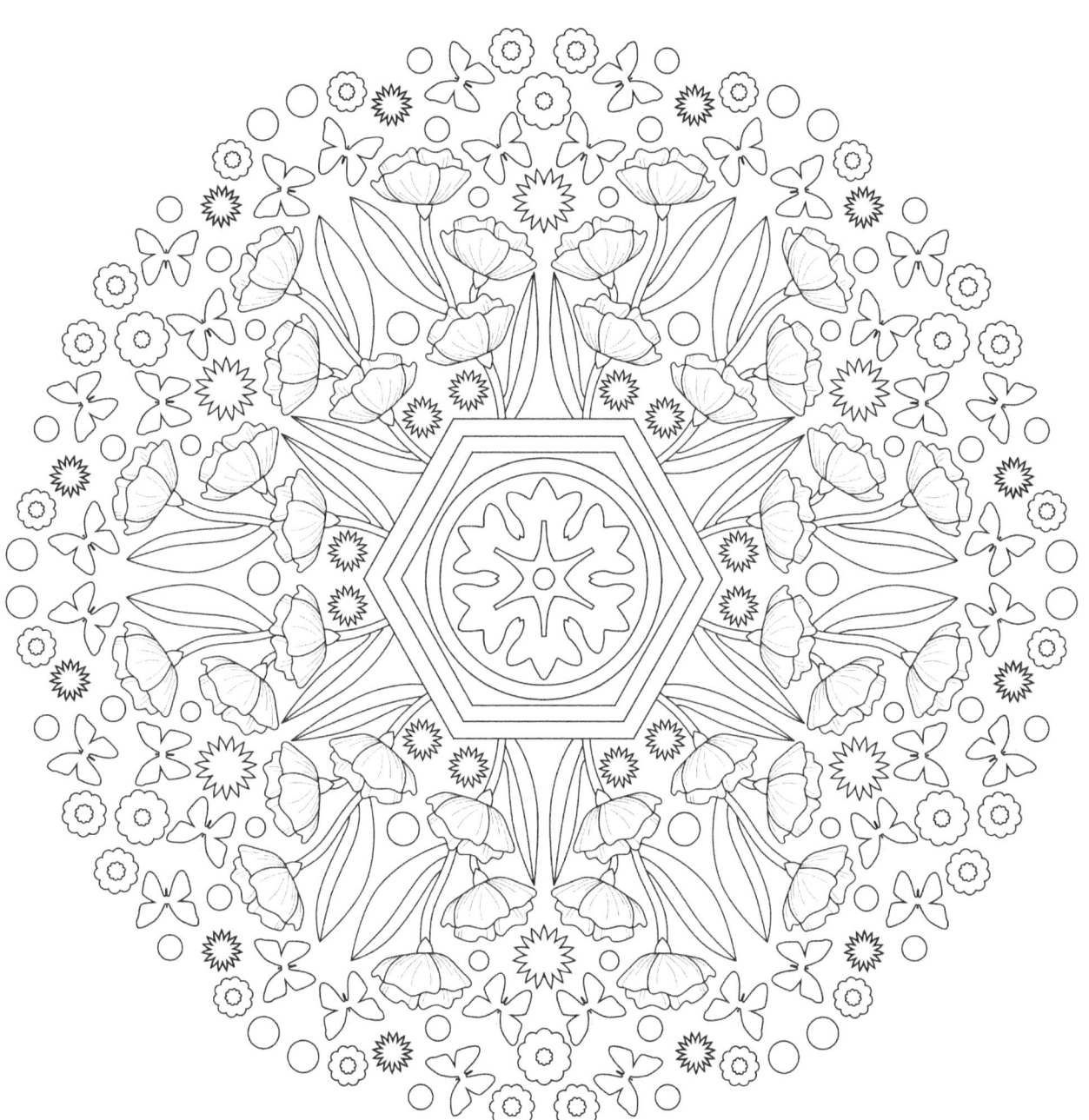

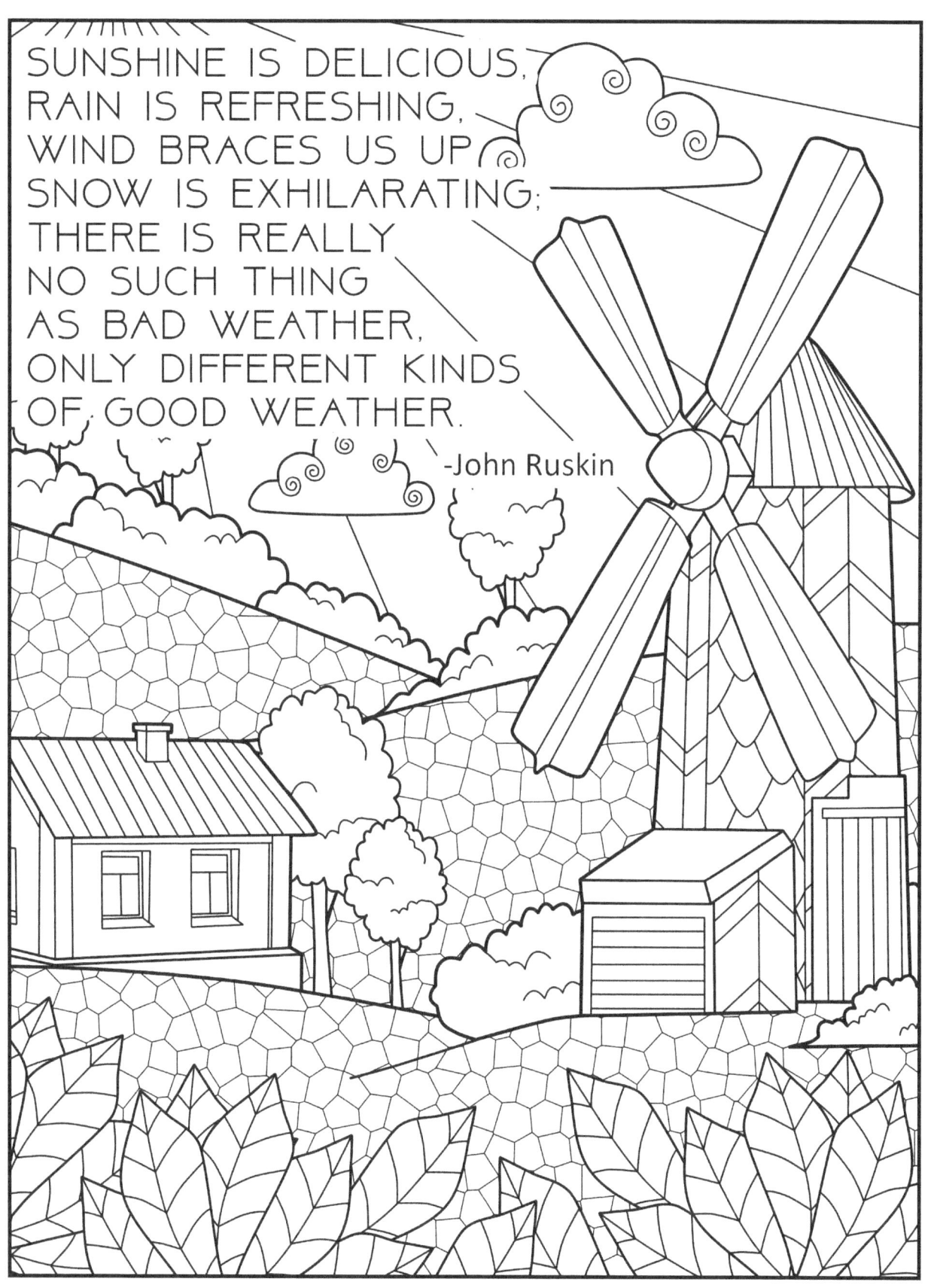

SUNSHINE IS DELICIOUS,
RAIN IS REFRESHING,
WIND BRACES US UP
SNOW IS EXHILARATING;
THERE IS REALLY
NO SUCH THING
AS BAD WEATHER,
ONLY DIFFERENT KINDS
OF GOOD WEATHER.

-John Ruskin

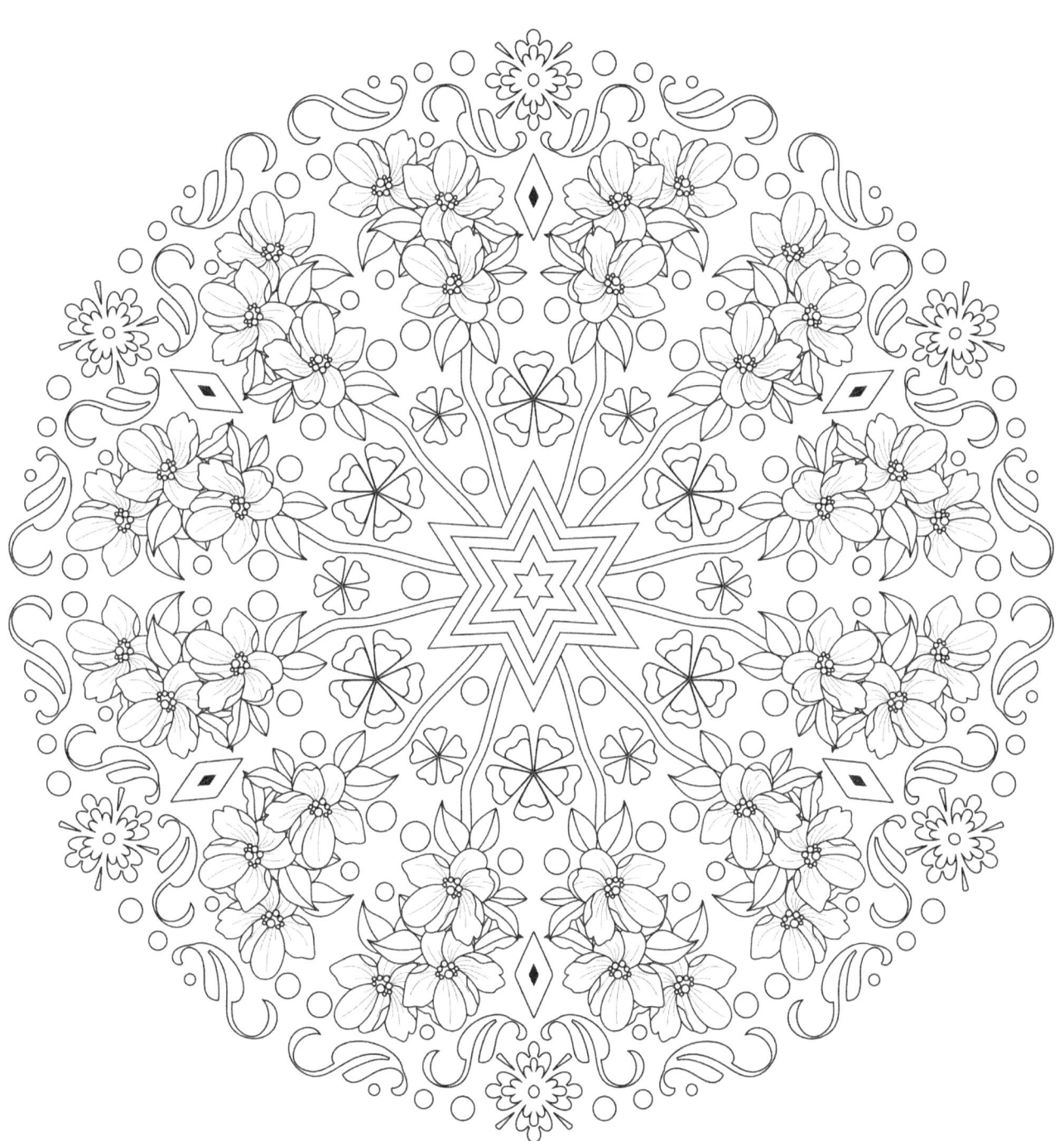

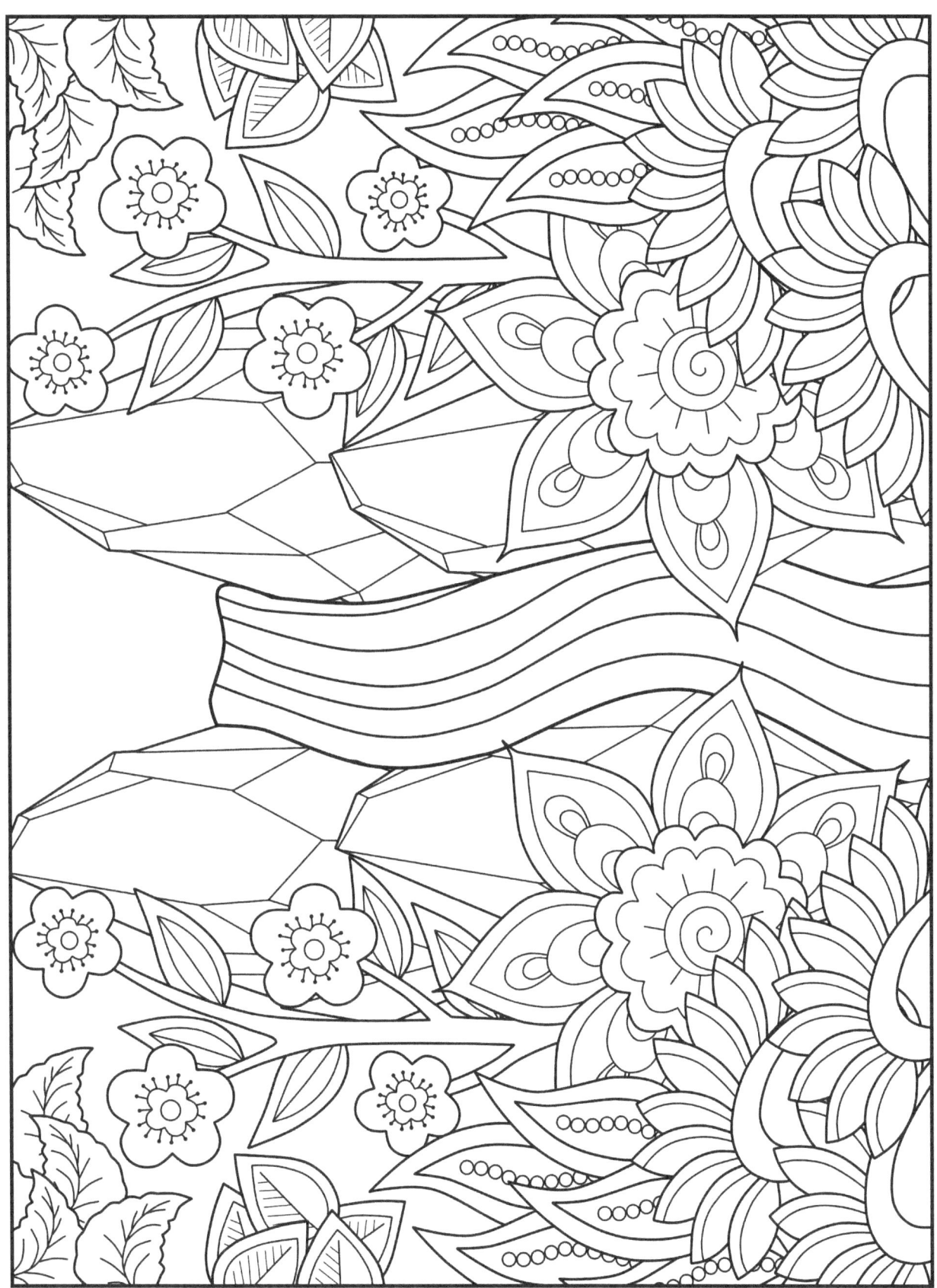

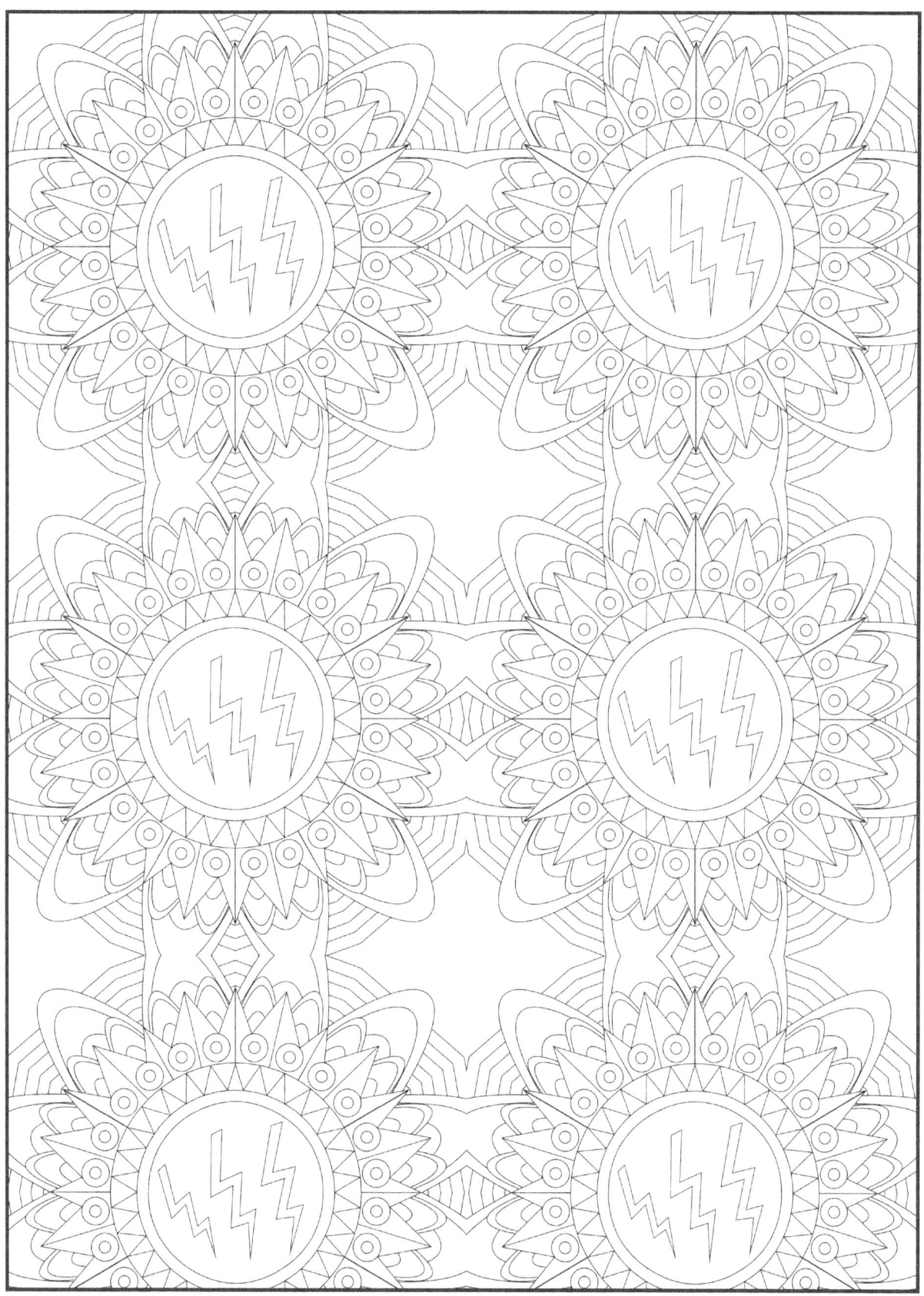

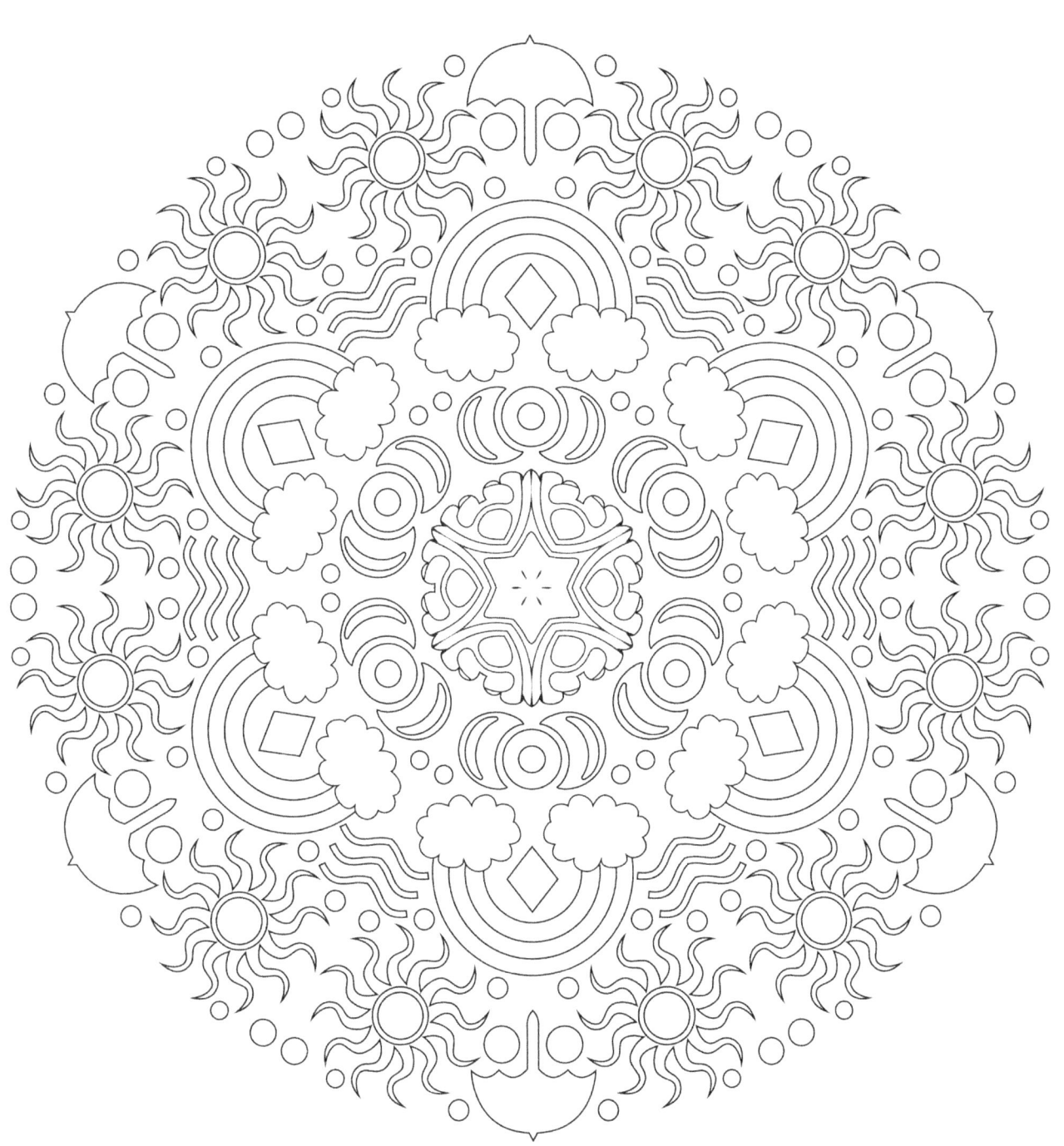

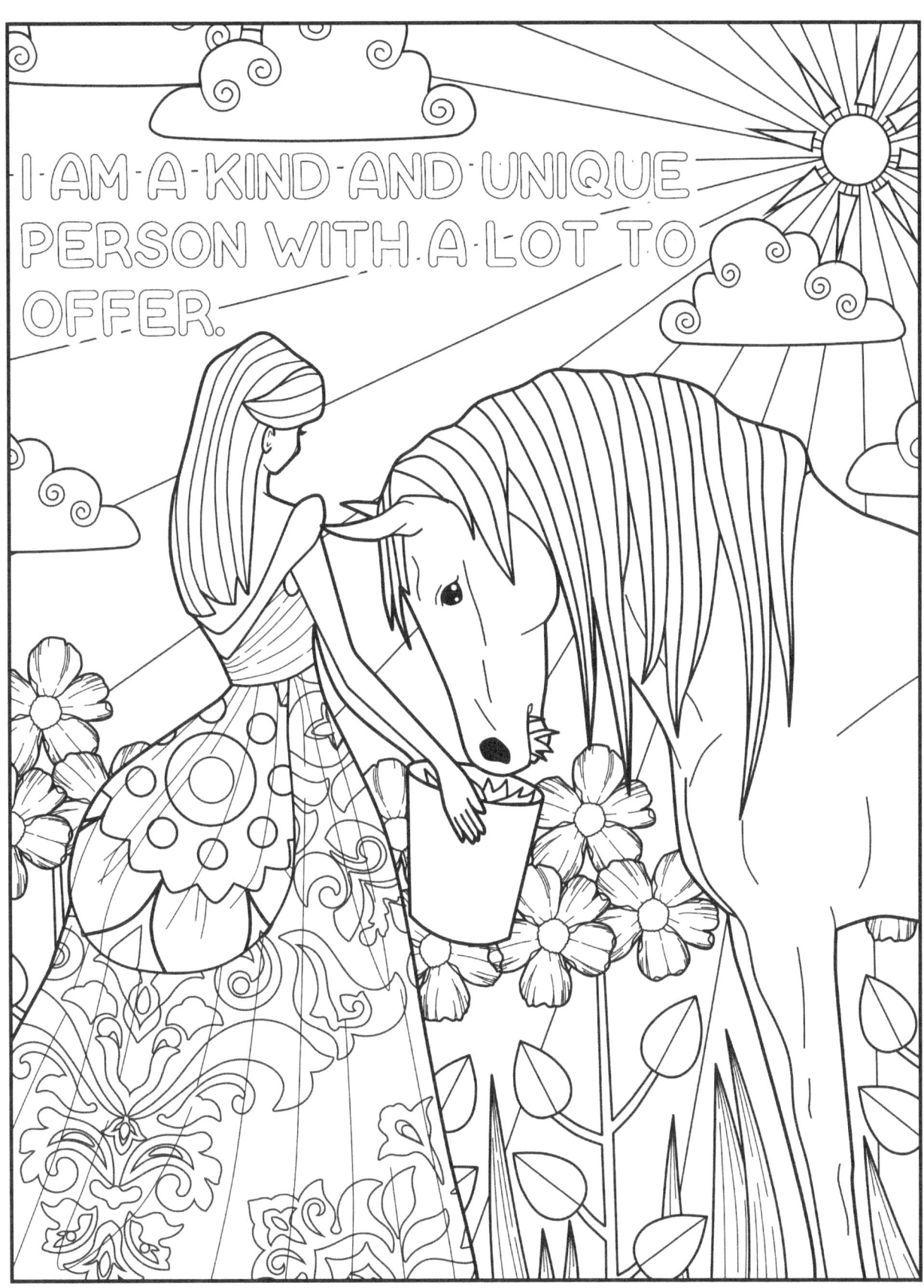

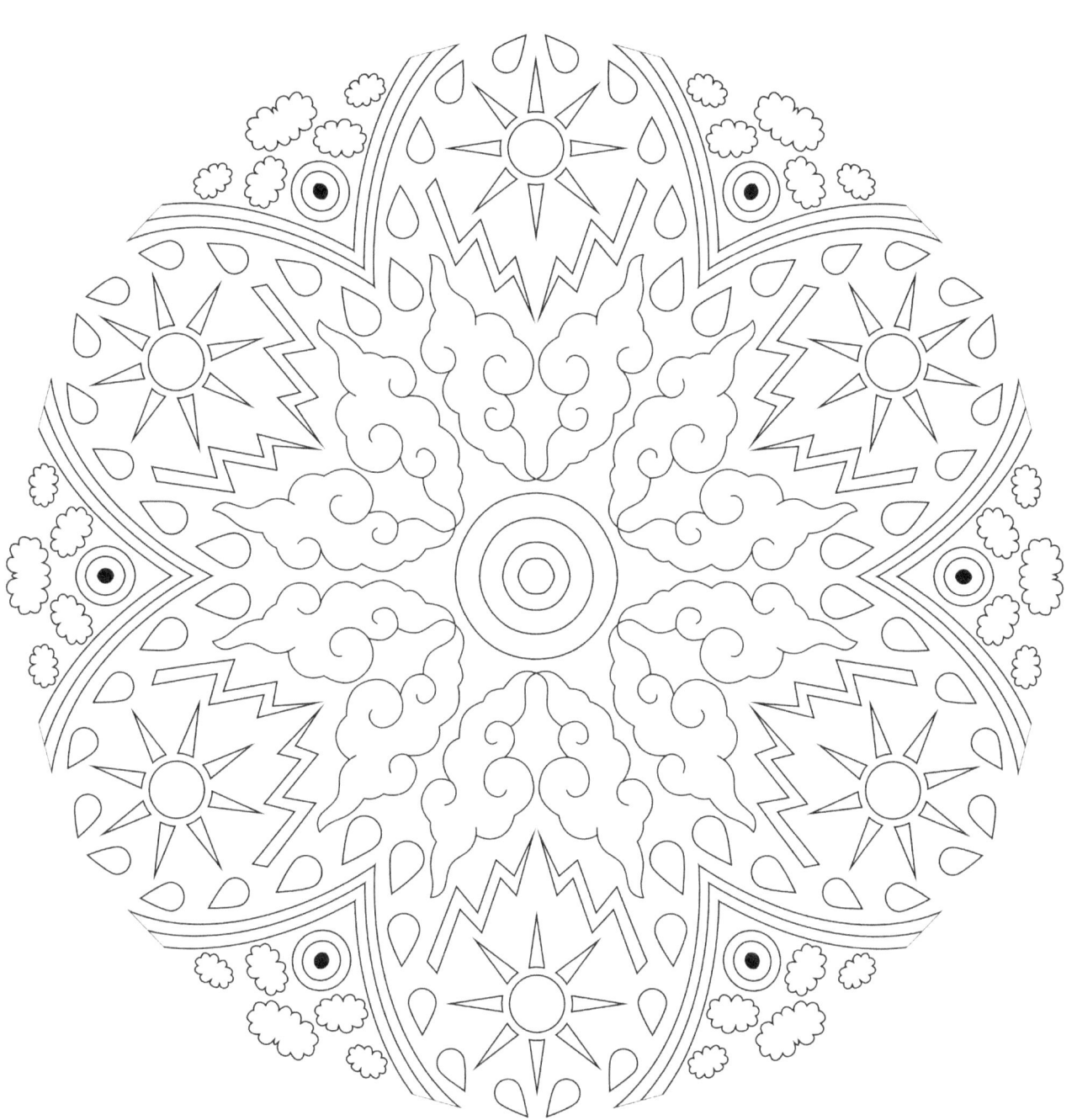

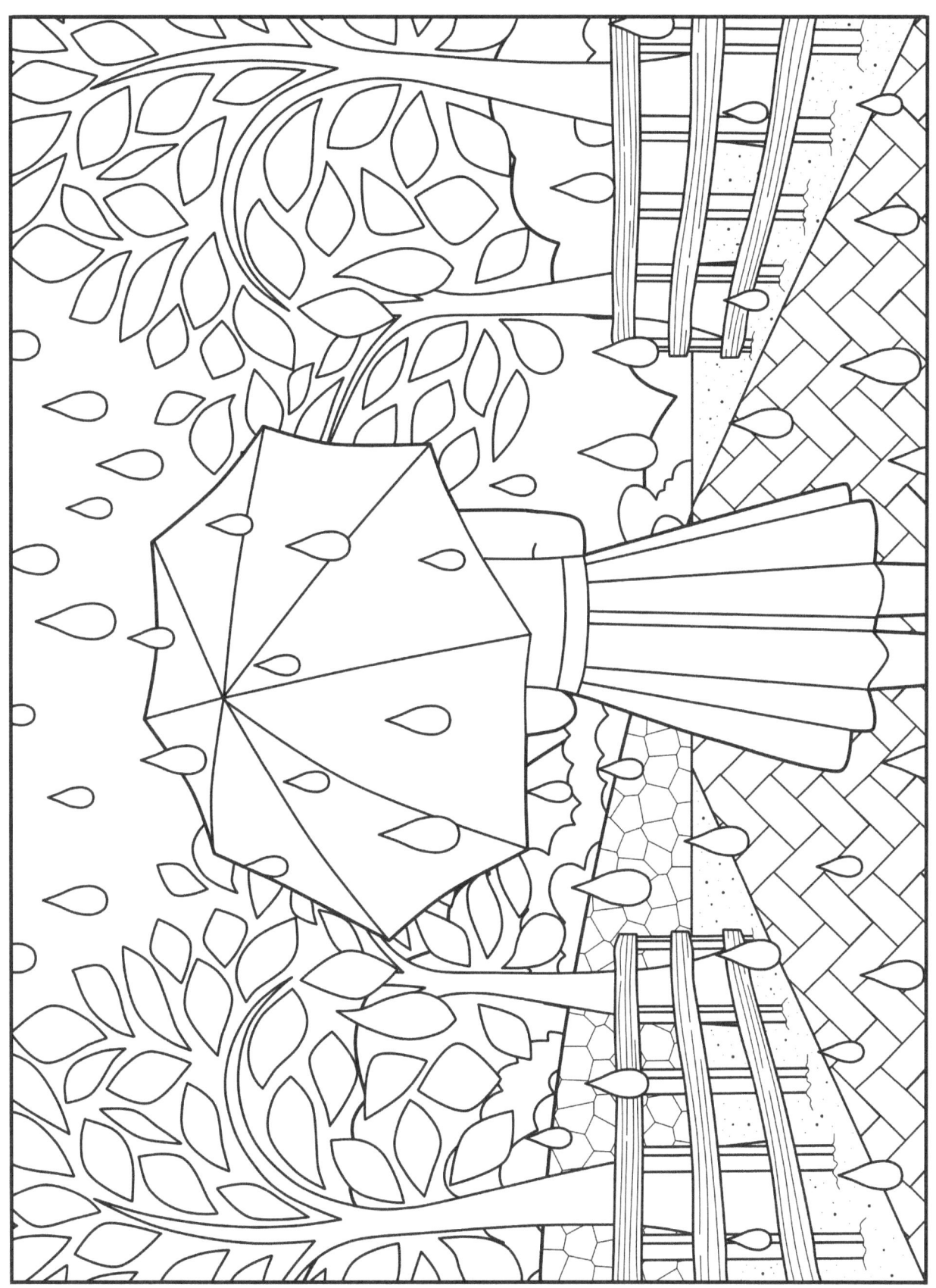

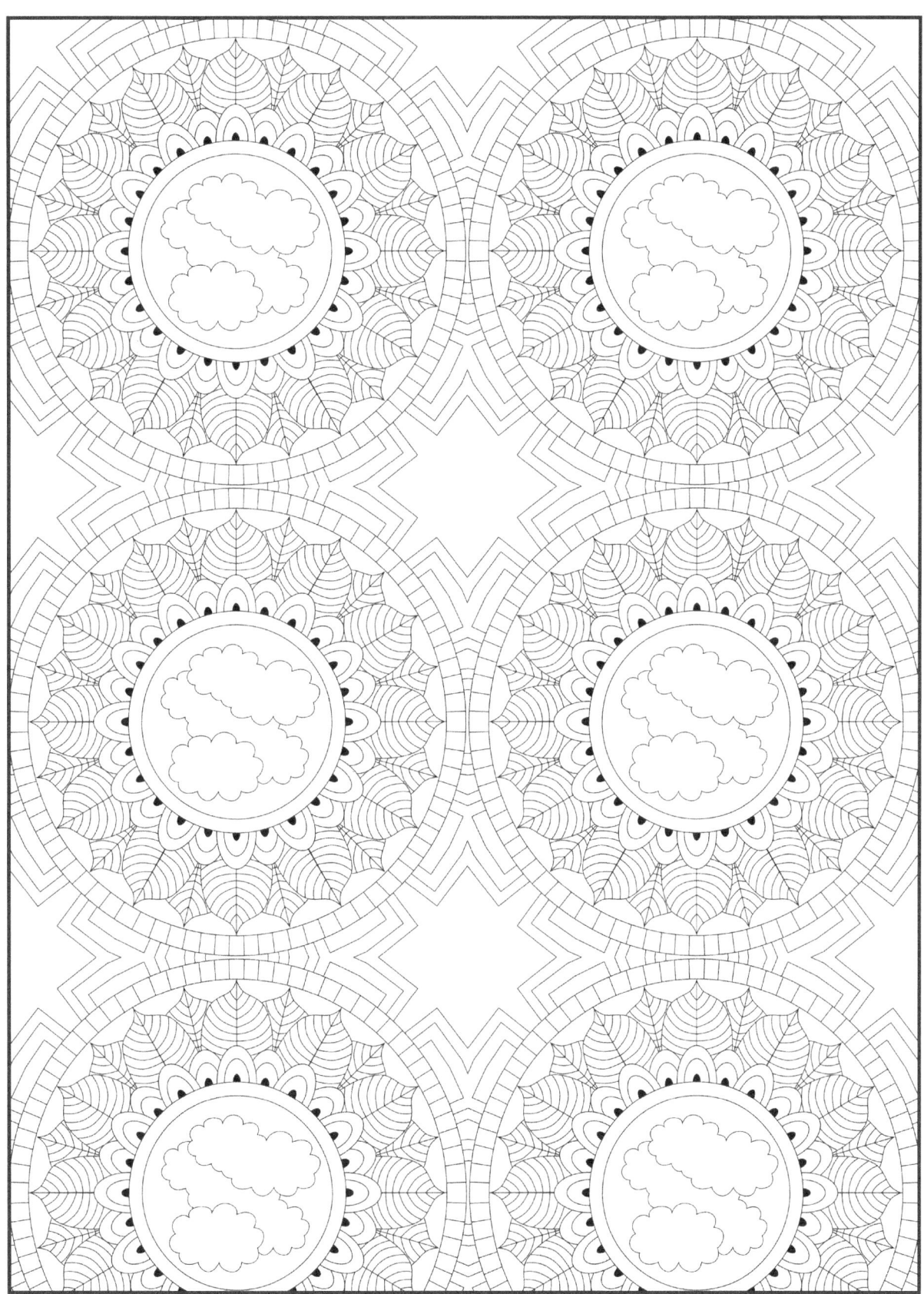

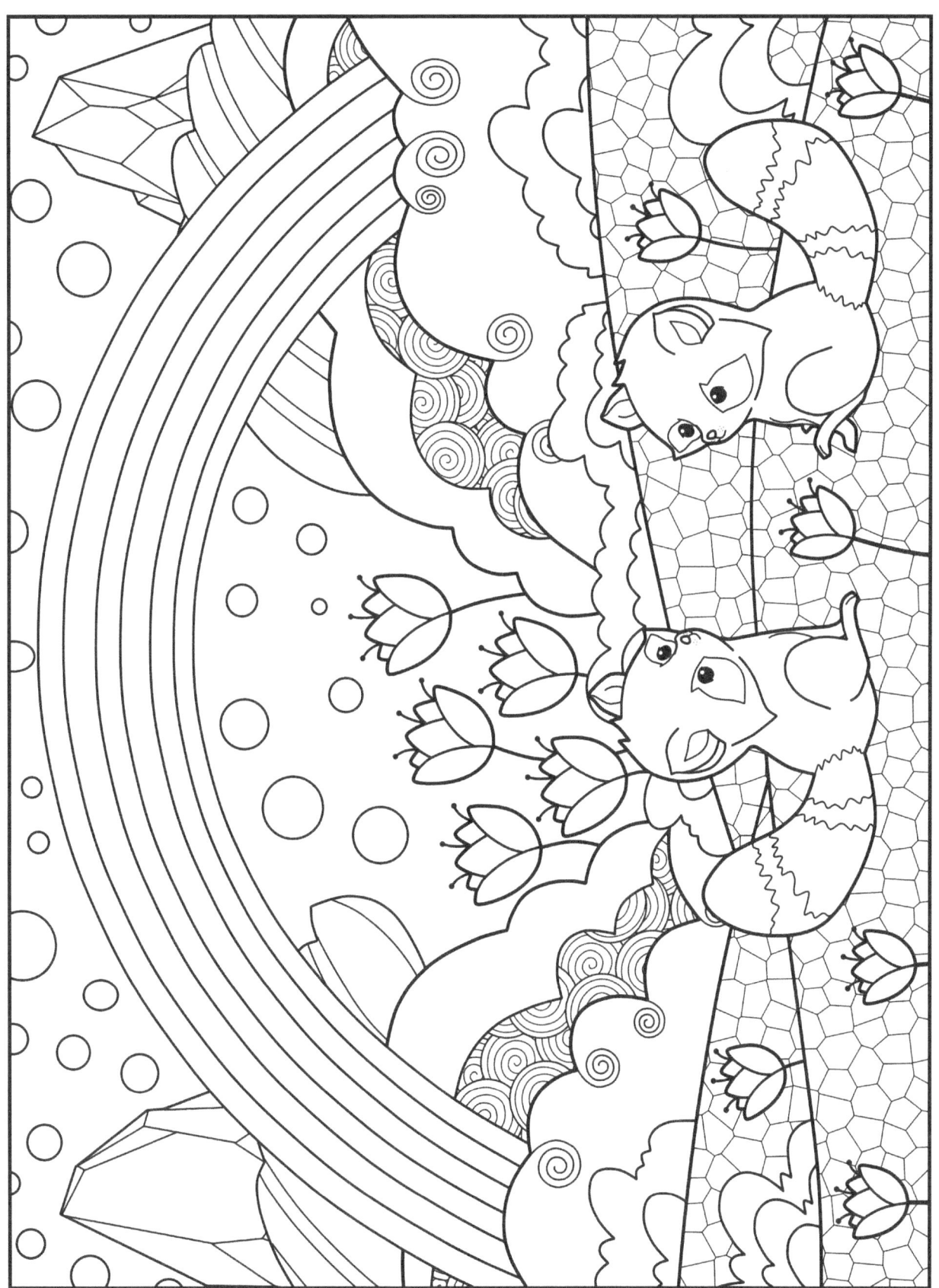

www.ingramcontent.com/pod-product-compliance
Lightning Source LLC
Chambersburg PA
CBHW081004220526
45467CB00008B/2691